INTRODUCTION

Whether you are weighing vegetables at the grocery store or mailing packages at the post office, you can turn your town into a teaching town just by making use of ordinary items in ordinary places.

Teaching Town is divided into eight chapters: Grocery Store, Post Office, Library, Hardware Store, Restaurant, Garden Store, Doctor's Office, and Gas Station.

Each chapter contains fun, easy activities to do at the location, followed by related activities that you and your child can do when you return home. The activities are grouped into the areas of language, creativity, thinking skills, coordination, science, and self-awareness.

At first glance, these activities may seem to be "just play." However, as the introductory sentences to the activities explain, each activity uses a specific skill—one that forms part of a foundation necessary for higher learning.

For instance, participating in dramatic-play and oral-language activities prepares your child for communicating clearly with others. Art projects spark the imagination needed for effective reading, writing, and scientific speculation. Playing matching and sorting games develops an understanding of likes and differences, a skill used in nearly all learning areas, including math, science, reading, and writing. Small-muscle coordination activities pave the way for learning how to use a pen or pencil; science activities promote thinking skills; and self-esteem activities lead to building self-confidence, so necessary for your child's success in all learning areas.

Since you are your child's first teacher, use the opportunity of daily outings to start teaching him or her basic skills and concepts. Just open to a page for one of the errands you plan to do today, skim through the easy step-by-step instructions, and begin!

A WORD ABOUT SAFETY

Keep in mind that when doing the activities, an adult should supervise to make sure that children do not put materials or objects into their mouths.

As for art materials, such as scissors, glue, or felt tip markers, use those that are specifically labeled as safe for children unless the materials are to be used only by an adult.

CONTENTS

GROCERY STORE 2	RESTAURANT 18
POST OFFICE 6	GARDEN STORE 22
LIBRARY 10	DOCTOR'S OFFICE 26
HARDWARE STORE 14	GAS STATION 30

GROCERY STORE

GROCERY PICTURE LIST
Your child will enjoy helping you shop with this prereading activity.

1) When writing your grocery list, select several items to put on a separate picture list for your child to use.
2) Draw a simple picture of each item on a piece of paper.
3) Indicate the quantity of each item by writing the number next to the picture or by drawing the picture that number of times.
4) At the store, give your child the list and a pen.
5) As you walk through the store, help your child find the pictured items, place them in the shopping cart, and check them off the list.

LETTERS EVERYWHERE
The grocery store is a great place to try this letter-recognition activity.

1) With your child, find a food package with the first letter of his or her name on it.
2) As you walk up and down the aisles, have your child look for other food packages that contain that letter.
3) Help your child find the letter on shelves, sale signs, or large signs overhead.
4) Follow the same procedure to look for other familiar letters.

Brighter Vision Publications   BV15011 Teaching Town

GROCERY STORE

COUPON MATCH
Let your child help you grocery shop with this matching activity.

1) Before going to the store, select several grocery coupons for products you want to buy.
2) Place the coupons in an envelope and give them to your child to carry.
3) When you get to the store, help your child look for the products that match the pictures on the coupons and place those items in the shopping cart.
4) Let your child give the coupons to the clerk when you reach the checkout stand.

ANOTHER IDEA: Let your child use crayons or felt tip markers to decorate the envelope for carrying coupons. Save the envelope to use on future trips to the store.

LARGE AND SMALL
Recognizing large and small sizes is part of this matching activity.

1) Take your child to the canned fruits or vegetables section.
2) From the shelf, take a large can and a small can of two different products, such as peaches and pineapple or beans and corn. (Make sure that each large and small can are from the same company and have matching labels.)
3) Mix up the cans and show them to your child.
4) Ask your child to find the large and small size of each canned product.
5) Replace the cans on the shelf and choose other sets of large and small cans, if you wish.

HOW MANY INSIDE?
Your child will become more aware of the number of items in a package with this math activity.

1) Take your child to the egg section.
2) Open an egg carton and count the number of eggs inside, or count as you and your child fill a carton with eggs to purchase later.
3) Point to another carton and ask your child to guess how many eggs will be inside.
4) Open the carton and have your child help count the eggs to check his or her response.
5) Follow the same procedure with other packaged items, such as hot dogs, canned or bottled sodas, or boxed juices. (Be sure to choose only those items that can be counted without destroying the packaging.)

GROCERY STORE

BAKERY FUN

This learning activity develops math skills as well as color-recognition skills.

1) Take your child to the bakery display case.
2) Encourage your child to name the kinds of items in the case, such as cookies, doughnuts, and cakes.
3) Ask your child to do such things as the following.
   - Count the number of bear cookies, jelly doughnuts, clown cupcakes, and so forth.
   - Name the shapes of different cookies.
   - Point to the yellow cakes, the green cookies, the doughnuts with red sprinkles, and so on.

ANOTHER IDEA: Let your child choose one bakery item and order it from the salesclerk to buy and take home.

IN-CART WAITING GAMES

This game uses language skills, math skills, color-recognition skills, and shape-recognition skills.

1) When you are waiting in line at the checkout stand, let your child sit in the shopping cart and do activities like those that follow.
   - Ask your child to point to and name each of the items in your cart.
   - With your child, count the number of items in the cart.
   - Have your child name a color that he or she is wearing. Ask him or her to point to items in the cart that are the same color.
   - Ask your child to find an item that is round, square, or rectangular.

I SEE SOMETHING

Try playing this problem-solving game while you are waiting in line with your child.

1) Select an item that you and your child can see.
2) Start describing the item to your child. For instance, if the item is a helium-filled birthday balloon, you might say, "I see something that floats in the air, is shiny, and has words on it."
3) Keep giving clues until your child guesses what the item is.
4) Let your child describe an item and have you guess what it is.

GROCERY STORE—AT HOME FUN

PLAYDOUGH BAKERY
This art activity is always popular with young children.

1) Set out playdough along with a rolling pin, cookie cutters, small pans, a muffin tin, and a baking sheet.
2) Have your child roll out some of the playdough, cut out cookie shapes, and place them on the baking sheet.
3) Let your child use the rest of the playdough to make such things as muffins or cakes to "bake" in a pretend oven.
4) When the baked goods are "done," let your child place them in bakery boxes, if you wish.

ANOTHER IDEA: Give your child such items as cookie sprinkles and birthday candles to use for decorating his or her baked goods.

BUYING AND SELLING
This simple activity helps develop math skills.

1) Select five empty food containers.
2) Using a pen, make five "price stickers" by writing the numbers 1 to 5 on plain stickers or pieces of masking tape.
3) Attach one price sticker to each food container.
4) Set out the containers and give your child 15 "dollar bills" cut from green paper.
5) Have your child identify the number on each container and give you that number of dollars to "buy" it.
6) When your child has purchased all the items, trade places and let your child be the seller.

AGE VARIATION: For younger children, attach one to five stickers to the food containers. Have the children count the stickers on a container and hand you that many dollars to buy it.

BAGGING GROCERIES
This activity helps your child practice making comparisons.

1) Set out a variety of grocery items, such as a melon, a plastic bottle of juice, several cans of food, a box of dry cereal, a package of cookies, and a bag of chips.
2) Give your child a large brown paper grocery bag.
3) Let your child pack the grocery items in the paper bag, one at a time.
4) Encourage your child to think about which items are heavier and which are lighter. Then have him or her decide which items should go in the bag last so that they do not get squashed or broken.
5) When the bag has been packed, let your child unpack it and help you put the items away.

POST OFFICE

POSTCARDS TO MAIL

This prereading-prewriting activity will encourage your child to keep an eye out for the mail carrier.

1) Before going to the post office, select a postcard to send to your child.
2) Let your child observe as you write a message, address the card, and stamp it.
3) Together, mail the postcard at the post office.
4) At home, watch with your child for the mail carrier to deliver the special mail.
5) Help your child "write" a postcard to mail to you.
6) Show your child the card when the mail carrier delivers it.

POSTCARD STORIES

Try this oral-language activity while you are waiting in line at the post office.

1) Have ready to mail several picture postcards that show familiar landmarks or other interesting scenes.
2) Give your child one of the postcards and ask him or her to describe the picture.
3) Give your child another postcard. Have him or her tell you how the picture is different from the one on the first postcard.
4) Ask your child to pretend that he or she is in one of the postcard pictures. Then have your child tell you what things he or she would like to do there.

ANOTHER IDEA: For a prewriting activity, help your child add his or her name to the postcards you are mailing.

POST OFFICE

STAMP DESCRIPTIONS

For this listening game, use stamps on display at the post office.

1) Show your child several different postage stamps.
2) Ask your child to listen carefully while you begin to describe one of the stamps.
3) When your child recognizes which stamp you are describing, have him or her point to that stamp.
4) Let your child describe one of the stamps for you to identify.

WHICH IS HEAVIER?

Try this math game at the post office when you have packages to mail.

1) Prepare two packages for the mail.
2) At the post office, let your child hold first one package, then the other.
3) Ask your child to tell you which package is heavier and which is lighter.
4) Have your child check his or her responses by watching the postal clerk weigh the packages.

ANOTHER IDEA: Ask your child which is heavier, a stamp or an apple? A shoe or a postcard? An envelope or a car?

FUN IN LINE

This math game provides an enjoyable way to pass the time while waiting in line at the post office.

1) Call attention to people in line at the post office.
2) Ask your child to point out who is first in line and who is last.
3) Have your child count the people in line in ways such as those below.
   - people with packages
   - people with letters
   - people with packages and letters

POST OFFICE

ARRANGING LETTERS

Do this ordering activity at the post office when you have a number of letters to mail.

1) Give your child several letters of different sizes.
2) Ask your child to place the largest letter on your outstretched hands or a flat surface.
3) One at a time, have your child place the remaining letters on top of the first one, arranging them from largest to smallest.

READY TO MAIL

This mailing activity helps develop eye-hand coordination.

1) At the post office, give your child several letters addressed for mailing and a matching number of postage stamps.
2) Show your child where the stamps belong on the envelopes.
3) Let your child lick the stamps and stick them on the letters.
4) Help your child mail the letters, one at a time, in the mail slot or a mailbox.

LETTER BALANCE

Try this activity, which promotes small-muscle development, when you are waiting in line.

1) Ask your child to hold out his or her hand, palm down.
2) Place a letter on the back of your child's hand.
3) Have your child see how long he or she can balance the letter without letting it fall.
4) Let your child try balancing the letter on the opposite hand.
5) Have your child place the letter on your hand for you to balance.

POST OFFICE—AT-HOME FUN

STAMP PICTURES

This art activity provides a creative way to reuse colorful postage stamps.

1) Cut different kinds of canceled stamps from their envelopes.
2) Give your child the stamps, along with a piece of plain paper, glue, and felt tip markers.
3) Have your child glue the stamps on the paper any way he or she wishes.
4) Let your child use the markers to create a design on the paper that incorporates the stamps.

ANOTHER IDEA: If you have a large number of stamps, let your child glue them all over a piece of paper to make a collage.

MAIL MATCHUPS

This matching activity uses eye-hand coordination skills.

1) Select four or five envelopes of different sizes.
2) For each envelope, cut an index card or a piece of heavy paper to fit exactly inside.
3) Set out the envelopes and cards.
4) Let your child try to fit the cards into the envelopes to find the matchups.
5) Keep the cards and envelopes in a large mailing envelope for your child to play with again another time.

STAMP LOTTO

Your child will enjoy playing this matching game.

1) Collect four different pairs of canceled postage stamps.
2) With a pen, divide two index cards into four sections each.
3) Glue one set of four postage stamps on one index card and the matching set of four stamps on the second card.
4) Cut one of the cards into four sections to make game pieces. Use the other card as a gameboard.
5) Mix up the game pieces and let your child place them on the matching sections of the gameboard.

AGE VARIATION: For older children, include six to eight sections on the gameboard and make six to eight matching game pieces.

LIBRARY

LOUD AND SOFT

Encourage appropriate library behavior with this vocabulary-building activity.

1) Before going to the library, talk with your child about loud and soft.

2) Find a music station on the radio. Turn the volume up and down, each time asking your child to tell you if the sound is loud or soft.

3) With your child, recite a nursery rhyme, such as "Mary Had a Little Lamb," first in a loud voice, then in a soft one.

4) Talk with your child about how soft voices are used at the library.

5) At the library, whenever necessary, use an agreed upon hand signal to remind each other to speak softly.

BOOK STORIES

Your child is sure to enjoy this prereading activity.

1) At the library, select a storybook that is unfamiliar to you and your child.

2) Together, "read" the book by looking at the illustrations and making up a story about what is in them.

3) Encourage your child to name the characters and describe what is happening in the illustrations.

4) After enjoying your own story, read the author's story with your child.

5) Ask your child to tell you which story he or she liked best.

Brighter Vision Publications

BV15011 Teaching Town

LIBRARY

BOOK QUESTIONS

This prereading activity helps make books come alive for your child.

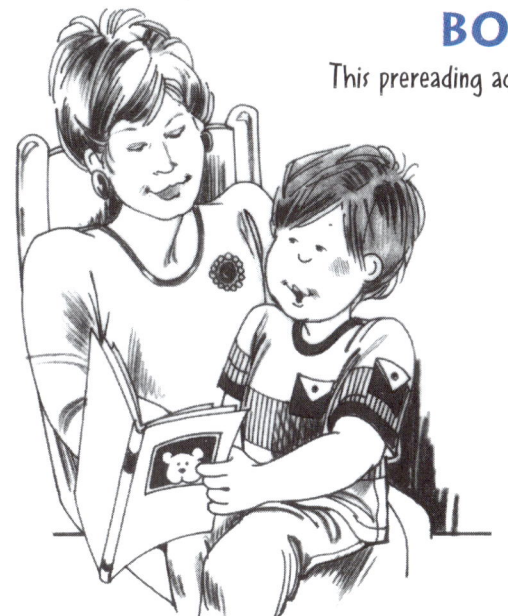

1) Choose a storybook at the library.
2) As you read the book to your child, stop frequently to ask questions such as the following.
   - "What would you do if you were the story character?"
   - "Why do you think he or she is sad?"
   - "What made him or her do that?"
   - "What do you think will happen next?"
3) Ask similar questions whenever you read storybooks to your child.

COLOR SEARCH

This color-recognition activity encourages your child to become more aware of book illustrations.

1) Choose a color such as red.
2) With your child, look through a library picture book you have selected together.
3) Ask your child to point to and name red things in each illustration.
4) Follow the same procedure with a different color.

PAGE COUNT

This math activity uses comparison skills.

1) Find two short picture books of different lengths.
2) With your child, count the pages first in one book, then in the other.
3) Ask your child to tell you which book has the most pages and which has the fewest.

ANOTHER IDEA: For a predicting activity, ask your child to guess which book will have the most pages before you count them.

LIBRARY

BOOK PILE
Encourage your child to help organize books on a library table with this ordering activity.

1) On a low library table, gather together four to six storybooks.
2) Ask your child to find the largest book and place it in front of you.
3) Have your child stack the remaining books on top of the first one from largest to smallest.

ABOUT ME
Use this self-esteem activity to help make the library experience a personal one for your child.

1) On each library visit try one or more of the following ideas.
   - Have your child look through books to find a picture of a child who looks like himself or herself.
   - Ask your child to name one or two favorite books. Look for them together and check them out.
   - Talk about subjects that interest your child. Have him or her ask the librarian to help find a book on one of the topics.

BOOK BINGO
This classification activity uses prereading skills.

1) Divide a large index card or piece of heavy paper into nine sections.
2) In each section, print a topic, such as one of the following: "Family, Cars, Snow, Bugs, Moon, Alphabet, Trains, Nursery Rhymes, Baby Animals."
3) Place the card, along with nine stickers, in a large envelope and take it with you when you go to the library.
4) Help your child find a book that relates to one of the topics listed on the card and read the book together.
5) When you have finished the book, let your child attach a sticker to the appropriate section on the card.
6) Continue the activity on other days until all the sections have stickers.

Brighter Vision Publications

BV15011 Teaching Town

LIBRARY—AT HOME FUN

TALKING BOOK

This listening activity provides your child with his or her own recording of a favorite storybook.

1) Place a blank audio tape in a small tape recorder.
2) Select a simple storybook.
3) Tape-record yourself reading the storybook. At the end of each page say, "It's time to turn the page now," or, "Please turn the page."
4) Show your child how to follow the words in the book while listening to the tape.
5) Let your child listen to the recorded story as often as he or she wishes.

SHELVING BOOKS

Encourage your child to organize his or her books with this classification activity.

1) Select a variety of your child's books.
2) Clear out a low shelf of a bookcase.
3) First, have your child arrange the books on the shelf by size.
4) Next, have your child arrange the books by color or by thickness.
5) Then, help your child arrange the books on the shelf by topic, such as animal books or books about transportation.
6) Have your child tell you which way of arranging the books he or she likes best.

MY PICTURE BOOK

This prereading activity is always a favorite with young children.

1) Make a blank book by stapling together several pieces of white paper with a colored construction paper cover.
2) With your child, choose a book topic such as animals.
3) Write the title "My Animal Book" and your child's name on the cover.
4) Have your child look through old magazines and catalogs to find pictures of animals.
5) Let your child cut or tear out the pictures and glue them in his or her book.
6) As your child "reads" the book to you, write his or her words on the pages, if you wish.

AGE VARIATION: Let younger children choose from precut pictures that you have placed in a box.

HARDWARE STORE

HARDWARE STORE COUNTING

A hardware store is a great place for doing math activities like this one.

1) As you walk down the aisles with your child, stop now and then to count items such as those below.
   - screwdrivers (or other small tools) in a package
   - mounted hardware pulls in a row
   - a handful of metal washers
   - paint cans on a shelf
   - plastic trash bins in a stack
2) Encourage your child to look for other items that he or she would like to count.

LETTER SEARCH

This activity helps develop letter recognition.

1) Take your child to the area of the store where press-on alphabet letters are displayed.
2) Ask your child to look for different letters, such as a B, an N, or a U.
3) Help your child find the letters in his or her name.

ANOTHER IDEA: For a math activity, point out the press-on numbers, asking your child to find a 2, a 5, and so forth.

HARDWARE STORE

BIGGEST AND SMALLEST
This comparison activity can also be done with nails, screws, and similar items.

1) At the store, show your child a display of tools, such as screwdrivers, that come in various sizes.
2) Ask your child to tell you which screwdriver is the biggest and which is the smallest.
3) Follow the same procedure with other tools, such as wrenches and hammers.

ANOTHER IDEA: Ask your child to point to the small, medium, and large size of a particular tool.

TOOL RIDDLES
You and your child will enjoy this problem-solving activity.

1) Show your child where tools are displayed in the store.
2) Name several of the tools and talk about how they are used.
3) Make up a riddle about one of the tools. For example, say, "I pound in nails. I have a wooden handle. What am I?" (hammer)
4) When your child answers the riddle, make up another one, or have your child make up a riddle for you to answer.

SORTING SCREWS
Your child will use matching and sorting skills when doing this activity.

1) In the store, find a low row of four or five bins that contain screws of different sizes.
2) Remove one screw from each bin, mix them up, and give them to your child.
3) Help your child put each screw back into the bin that contains screws of the same size.

HARDWARE STORE

HOW DO THEY FIT?

This activity helps promote small-muscle development.

1) In the plumbing section of the store, look for bins of plastic fittings.
2) Remove several of the fittings that go together.
3) Let your child practice screwing the fittings together and unscrewing them.
4) Have your child help you put the fittings back into the proper bins.

ANOTHER IDEA: Follow the same procedure using extra-large nuts and bolts.

DOORMAT TEXTURES

This sensory-awareness activity involves recognition of different textures.

1) Take your child to the area of the store where doormats are displayed.
2) Arrange three doormats with different textures in a row on the floor.
3) Have your child touch the mats and tell you which feels smooth, soft, prickly, and so forth.
4) While your child closes his or her eyes, move the mats around and ask your child to try to identify them by touch.
5) Replace the doormats where you found them.

COLORS AND FEELINGS

Try this self-esteem activity when you are in the paint section of the store.

1) Select paint sample strips of different colors.
2) Show the strips to your child.
3) Have your child tell you which colors make him or her feel happy, sad, excited, restful, and so forth.
4) Ask questions such as: "If you could paint the walls of your room any color you wanted, what color would you choose? What color would you paint the floor? The ceiling? The furniture?"

ANOTHER IDEA: For a matching game, let your child help you put the paint sample strips back into the display case with the strips that contain matching colors.

HARDWARE STORE—AT-HOME FUN

FIX-IT PERSON
This dramatic-play activity promotes coordination and thinking skills.

1) Select a sturdy box to use as a fix-it box for your child.

2) In the box, place items such as screwdrivers, large screws, plastic foam pieces, a tape measure, old locks and keys, broken toys, and masking tape.

3) Let your child pretend to be Mr. or Ms. Fix-It, and do such things as drive screws into the plastic foam pieces, measure furniture or other objects, match the locks and keys, and "repair" the broken toys with masking tape.

4) Can your child think of other "fix-it projects" to do? What about using a dry paintbrush to "paint" furniture?

COLOR SHADES
This ordering activity uses color-recognition skills.

1) Bring home from a hardware store several paint sample strips of different colors.

2) Cut each shaded strip into separate color pieces and place the pieces of each strip in a separate envelope.

3) Let your child remove the color pieces from one envelope and arrange them in order from lightest to darkest.

4) Have your child follow the same procedure with the color pieces in the other envelopes.

5) Let your child put the pieces back into the envelopes to play with again another time.

HOME REPAIR SEQUENCE CARDS
Understanding what comes first, next, and last is the focus of this sequencing activity.

1) Select three index cards.

2) Using felt tip markers, draw three simple pictures on the cards that show the steps in repairing a broken table; for instance, a table with two legs, the same table with three legs, the table with four legs.

3) Make similar sets of sequence cards to show the steps in other home repair jobs, such as changing a light bulb or painting the front of a house.

4) Store each set of cards in a separate envelope.

5) To play, let your child remove the cards from an envelope and arrange them in the proper order.

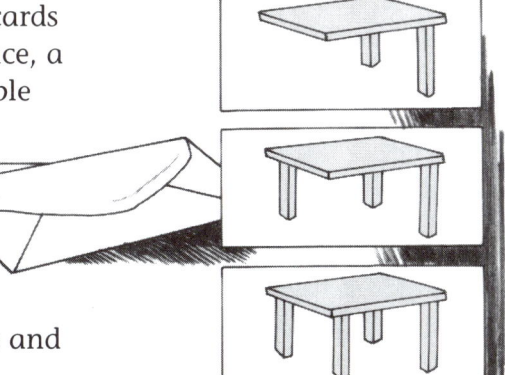

RESTAURANT

NAPKIN PUPPET

This oral-language activity can be done at the restaurant while you are waiting to be served.

1) To make a puppet, first cover your hand with a paper napkin.
2) Bring your thumb and fingers together and gently push in the napkin between them to form a mouth.
3) Let your child use a pen to add eyes and other details.
4) Use the puppet to talk to your child about what is going on at the restaurant, what you are going to order, and so forth.

ANOTHER IDEA: Make a second Napkin Puppet for your child and have your puppets talk to each other.

STRAW SOUNDS

Try this listening activity when you are at a fast-food restaurant.

1) Hold a drinking straw in a glass of water placed on the table.
2) Have your child listen as you blow across the top of the straw to make a sound.
3) Continue blowing as you lower the straw into the water. Ask your child to tell you what happens to the sound. (It becomes higher.)
4) Continue blowing as you raise the straw in the water. What happens to the sound now? (It becomes lower.)
5) Let your child try creating high and low sounds with his or her own glass of water and drinking straw.

RESTAURANT

PLACEMAT BOARD GAME
This matching activity can also be done with numbers or alphabet letters.

1) Use the back of a paper placemat or a piece of scrap paper to make a gameboard.
2) Down the left-hand side of the gameboard, draw a column of shapes, such as a circle, a square, a triangle, a rectangle, and a star.
3) Down the right-hand side, draw the same shapes in a different order.
4) Let your child draw lines on the gameboard to connect the matching shapes.

PLACE SETTING MATCH
Your child reproduces a pattern with this learning game.

1) Sit next to your child at the restaurant table.
2) Arrange your knife, fork, spoon, and napkin in the proper places in front of you.
3) Place your child's silverware and napkin in a pile.
4) Ask your child to copy the arrangement of your place setting to create one for himself or herself.

ANOTHER IDEA: Arrange silverware pieces in a place setting on the back of a paper placemat and trace around them with a pen. Let your child place the silverware on the matching tracings.

PAPER WIGGLY WORM
This science activity is always entertaining for young children.

1) Stand a straw in its wrapper upright on the table.
2) Tear off the top of the wrapper.
3) Push the wrapper down around the straw as far as it will go.
4) Pull out the straw and set it aside, leaving the accordion-folded "worm" on the table.
5) Help your child shake one small drop of water at a time on the paper worm and watch as it "squirms" and "wiggles."
6) Explain that the drops of water make the tiny folds in the paper unfold, causing the wrapper to move around.

RESTAURANT—AT-HOME FUN

LET'S PLAY RESTAURANT
Your child will enjoy waiting tables with this dramatic-play activity.

1) On a table, let your child arrange such items as placemats, silverware, plates, and cups to make a pretend restaurant.
2) Provide a real menu or use one that you and your child design yourselves.
3) With your child, take turns being the server and the customer, doing such things as "reading" the menu, "writing" pretend orders on a notepad, and serving and enjoying imaginary foods.

FAST-FOOD ORDERS
Listening to and following directions is the focus of this activity.

1) From a fast-food restaurant, collect several hamburger containers, paper cups, and French fry holders, or cut out paper shapes to represent the three items.
2) Place the containers and a paper bag on a table.
3) Give your child an "order" to fill, such as one burger, two soft drinks, and one order of fries.
4) Have your child repeat your order as he or she places the appropriate containers or paper shapes into the bag.
5) Remove the items from the bag and continue the game, letting your child take a turn giving you an order to fill.

AGE VARIATION: For younger children, start by giving an order that includes just two items. For older children, include more items per order or ask for a larger number of each item.

MEASURING SOFT DRINKS
This math activity provides an entertaining way to develop measuring skills.

1) From a fast-food restaurant, collect a small, a medium, and a large paper cup (or use any small, medium, and large cups you have on hand).
2) Provide your child with water and a set of plastic measuring cups.
3) Let your child practice pouring and measuring to discover how much "soft drink" each cup holds.

RESTAURANT—AT-HOME FUN

COUNTING FRIES
This homemade math game can be used for various counting activities.

1) Collect two cardboard French fry holders of different sizes from a fast-food restaurant.
2) Using scissors, cut yellow sponges into French fry shapes.
3) Ask your child to count the number of fries that will fit into each holder.
4) Have your child remove the fries from each holder, counting as he or she does so.
5) Ask your child to fill each container with a specific number of fries.
6) Let your child make up other counting games to play using the fries and holders.

FOODS ON PLATES
Learning to understand ordinal numbers is the focus of this math activity.

1) Cut pictures of foods from old magazines and give them to your child.
2) Place three to five paper plates in a row.
3) Talk with your child about the positions of the plates—which one is first, second, and so on.
4) Have your child place the food pictures on the plates as you give directions such as: "Put the apple on the second plate. Put the sandwich on the third plate. Put the cake on the first plate."

MAY I TAKE YOUR ORDER?
This activity encourages self-esteem by letting your child help out at mealtime.

1) On a piece of paper, draw simple pictures of the beverages that will be offered at your next family meal.
2) After each picture, draw a box for each member of your family.
3) Give the "beverage menu" to your child.
4) At mealtime, have your child ask each person what drink he or she would like.
5) Have your child check off the drinks that each person requests.
6) Let your child bring the menu to the kitchen and help you prepare the beverages that were ordered.

GARDEN STORE

GARDENING TOOLS GAME

This dramatic-play activity will help your child learn about how garden tools are used.

1) Take your child to the area in the store where gardening tools are displayed.
2) Point to a tool, such as a hoe or rake, and help your child say its name.
3) Talk about how the tool is used.
4) Have your child pretend to hold the tool and act out how he or she would use it in a garden.

BUYING A PLANT

Your child will enjoy doing this oral-language activity.

1) With your child, look at small plants that are on display in the store.
2) Let your child choose a plant to purchase and take home.
3) Teach your child the plant's name.
4) Have your child take the plant to the salesclerk and ask how to care for it at home.
5) Later, discuss with your child what the clerk said about taking care of the plant.

ANOTHER IDEA: Make a weekly chart that shows when your plant should be watered. With your child, check off the task on the chart as you do it.

GARDEN STORE

SEED PACKET FUN

Colorful seed packets are great to use for matching activities like this one.

1) At the store, take your child to the seed packet display.
2) Talk with your child about the pictures of different flowers and vegetables on the packets.
3) Have your child close his or her eyes while you remove one of the seed packets from the display case.
4) Ask your child to open his or her eyes.
5) Give your child the seed packet and have him or her put it back into the display case with the packets that contain matching pictures.
6) Follow the same procedure using other seed packets.

ANOTHER IDEA: For a color-recognition game, have your child point to a seed packet that has a picture of red flowers, yellow squash, green lettuce, and so forth.

USING MY SENSES

This sensory-awareness activity is especially suited to a garden store.

1) Talk with your child about our five senses of sight, hearing, touch, smell, and taste.
2) Ask your child to look around and describe a special sight, such as a red geranium, for you.
3) Ask your child to listen and then name a sound, such as water flowing in a fountain.
4) Have your child touch and describe a textured item, such as a rough tree trunk or a smooth ceramic planter.
5) Ask your child to describe some scents, such as those given out by herbs or flowers.
6) Later, for a taste experience, let your child sample herbs that you have taken home and washed.

GARDENING BOX

This dramatic-play activity can be done either inside or outdoors.

1) Find a sturdy box.
2) In the box, place gardening items for your child to play with, such as a watering can, a trowel, gardening gloves, and empty seed packets.
3) Let your child use the gardening items to pretend he or she is planting a garden, watering the plants, and pulling weeds.
4) Ask your budding gardener to describe his or her garden for you.

GARDEN STORE—AT-HOME FUN

GARDEN PLAN
Encourage your child's imagination with this art activity.

1) From old seed catalogs, let your child cut or tear pictures of flowers, vegetables, and other plants.

2) Give your child a piece of brown construction paper or wrapping paper to use as an empty garden bed.

3) Have your child try arranging the flower and vegetable pictures on the paper in different ways to come up with a "garden" he or she likes.

4) When your child is satisfied with an arrangement, let him or her glue the pictures in place on the paper.

5) Display the Garden Plan on a wall or door for everyone to admire.

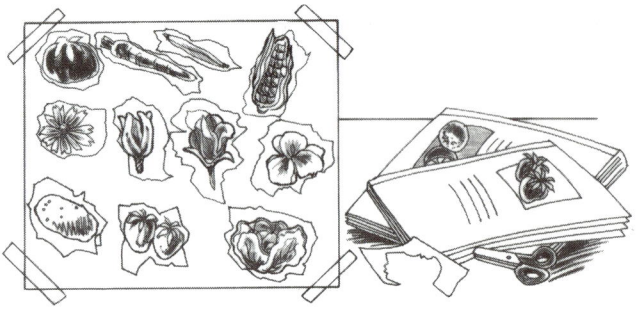

CITRUS SEED GARDENS
This natural science activity uses seeds of everyday fruits.

1) Have on hand potting soil and small flower pots.

2) Save several seeds from an orange, a lemon, or a grapefruit.

3) Help your child plant the seeds about 1 inch deep in a pot filled with potting soil. Gently add water.

4) Place the pot in a sunny spot, letting your child water the seeds a little every day.

5) Plant seeds from several different citrus fruits in separate pots and group them together to make a "garden."

HINT: Do not let the seeds dry out before planting or they may not sprout.

WHAT DO PLANTS NEED?
Try this science experiment to show that plants need sunlight in order to grow.

1) Let your child plant bean seeds in two pots of soil.

2) When the seeds have sprouted, let your child help place one pot in a sunny place, such as a window, and the other in a dark place, such as a closet.

3) Water both plants regularly.

4) After about two weeks, have your child compare the two plants. What has happened to the plant in the dark closet? (It has become pale and thin because it lacked sunlight.)

5) Let your child place the pale plant in a sunny spot, continue watering it, and observe over the coming days as it turns green.

ANOTHER IDEA: Have your child grow two plants in a sunny spot and experiment with watering one but not the other. What happens to the unwatered plant? (It becomes droopy.) Start watering the second plant and watch it perk up.

GARDEN STORE—AT-HOME FUN

FUN-TO-GROW PLANTS
This natural science activity offers ideas for growing edible plants.

1) Give your child space outdoors in a garden or planter to plant seeds that are easy to grow. Here are some suggestions.
   - Plant lettuce seeds along with spinach seeds to make a salad garden.
   - Grow several different herbs, such as oregano, chives, and thyme. Use the herbs in salads, on steamed vegetables, or on top of pizza.
   - Plant carrot and radish seeds to grow vegetables that taste terrific right out of the garden.
   - Plant sunflower seeds and watch the flowers grow to maturity. Harvest the seeds later.

2) Help your child care for his or her garden, watering and weeding as needed.

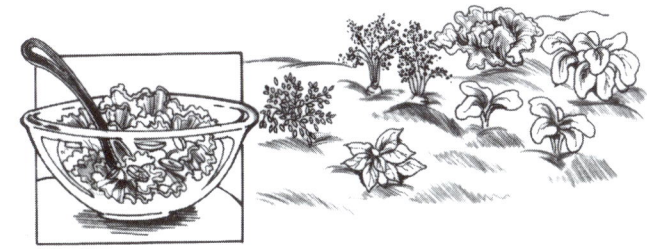

HOMEMADE TERRARIUM
Your child will enjoy growing plants in a different way with this natural science activity.

1) Put a layer of pebbles and 2 or 3 inches of potting soil in the bottom of a wide-mouthed glass or plastic jar.
2) Let your child help plant one or two small plants in the soil.
3) Have your child use a spoon to add a small amount of water to the plants.
4) Screw the lid on the jar.
5) Keep the terrarium in a spot where it will get plenty of light (but not in direct sunlight) and have your child observe as the plants grow.
6) Explain to your child that the water inside the terrarium is recycled over and over again so that no more water needs to be added.

> **HINT:** At first you may need to leave the lid off the jar for a while or add a little more water to get the right balance of moisture in the terrarium.

> **ANOTHER IDEA:** Let your child place a small plastic or ceramic animal in the terrarium, if he or she wishes.

FLOWER POT FUN
This ordering activity is enjoyable and easy to do.

1) Find four to six plastic flower pots that fit together, one inside the other.
2) Let your child help wash and dry the pots.
3) Encourage your child to practice nesting the pots together and taking them apart again.

DOCTOR'S OFFICE

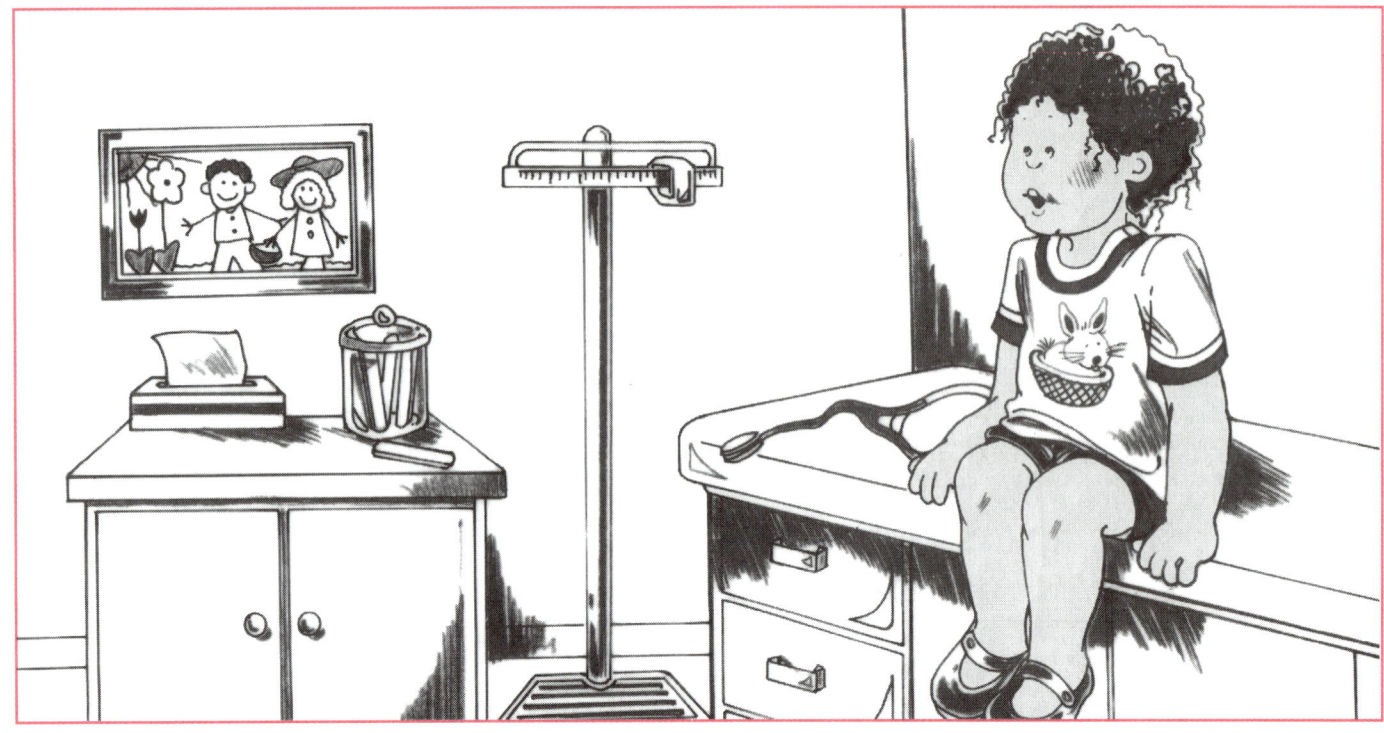

DOCTOR VISIT

Do this oral-language activity before your child's first visit to a new doctor.

1) Make arrangements to take your child to the doctor's office for a "learning visit."
2) Ask to have someone show you and your child around the office and introduce the doctor and nurse.
3) Help your child prepare in advance any questions he or she may have for the doctor. Make sure any fears are addressed.
4) If possible, arrange for your child to receive a disposable face mask or similar item to take home.
5) Later, talk about the visit, asking your child to tell you some of the new things he or she learned at the doctor's office.

COUNTING FUN

This math activity provides an entertaining way to pass the time while you are waiting.

1) With your child, count objects and people in the doctor's waiting room. Here are some examples.
   - number of chairs
   - number of people waiting
   - number of pictures on the wall
   - number of magazines
   - number of children's books
2) Have your child find other things to count.

DOCTOR'S OFFICE

PICTURE COLORS

This color-recognition activity involves observation skills.

1) Call attention to a picture on the wall of the waiting room or examining room.
2) Talk with your child about what he or she sees in the picture.
3) Ask your child questions such as: "What color is the dog? Is the boat blue or green? What red things can you see in the picture? How many yellow things can you see?"
4) Encourage your child to ask you a color question about a picture on the wall.

WHICH IS BIGGER?

Play this comparing game while you're waiting with your child in the examining room.

1) Help your child name various items in the room, such as the examining table, scale, stethoscope, and tongue depressors.
2) Ask questions such as: "Which is bigger, the stethoscope or a tongue depressor? The examining table or the scale?"
3) Continue with questions about other items. For instance, ask: "Which is bigger, a baby or a nurse? A bed or a hospital? An ambulance or a bandage?"
4) Let your child make up similar questions for you to answer.

PARTS OF THE BODY

This body-awareness activity is very appropriate for the doctor's office.

1) Give your child a compact or hand mirror.
2) Have your child look in the mirror and point to parts of his or her face, such as eyes, nose, lips, and teeth, as you name them.
3) Name other body parts, one at a time, and have your child point to those parts.

ANOTHER IDEA: With your child, find a picture of a person in a magazine. As you name different body parts, have your child point to them in the picture.

DOCTOR'S OFFICE—AT-HOME FUN

DOCTOR/NURSE BAG

Your child takes the role of doctor or nurse with this dramatic-play activity.

1) Find an old shaving kit or purse for your child to use as a doctor or nurse bag.
2) Inside the bag, place a few medical items, such as adhesive bandages, gauze strips, tongue depressors, cotton swabs, and cotton balls.
3) Give your child the bag and let him or her act out being a doctor or nurse, treating you or toy animal "patients" for various pretend ailments.

AGE VARIATION: Give older children notepads and pencils and encourage them to "write" prescriptions for their patients.

SHARING BOXES

Your child will learn good health habits with this sorting activity.

1) Using a felt tip marker, label one box with a happy face and the words "Alright to share" and another box with a sad face and the words "Not healthy to share."
2) Collect several familiar items that are alright to share with friends, such as a ball, a crayon, a toy, and a book, and several items that are not healthy to share, such as a toothbrush, a cup, a comb, and a straw.
3) Show your child two of the items, such as the ball and the toothbrush.
4) Talk about which item would not be healthy to share and why. (The toothbrush would not be healthy to share because it is something people put in their mouth.)
5) Mix up all the items and place them by the boxes.
6) Let your child choose one item at a time, tell you if it is alright to share or not, and then put the item into the appropriate box.

HELP FOR OUCHES

Your child will love this art activity.

1) Give your child a piece of construction paper along with crayons or felt tip markers.
2) Help your child draw a self-portrait with several "ouches" on its body.
3) Show your child how to unwrap some small adhesive bandages.
4) Let your child attach the bandages over the "ouches" in his or her picture.

DOCTOR'S OFFICE—AT-HOME FUN

GOOD HEALTH POSTERS
This art activity helps reinforce good health habits.

1) Let your child make Good-Health Posters to put up in his or her room.
2) On separate pieces of construction paper, use a dark crayon to write the titles "I Wash My Hands," "I Brush My Teeth," and "I Use a Tissue."
3) Let your child use crayons to add decorations.
4) Have your child complete the posters by taping or gluing a soap bar wrapper to the first paper, a flattened toothpaste box to the second paper, and a facial tissue to the third paper.
5) Display the finished posters on a wall or door.

ANOTHER IDEA: Title another poster "Do Not Touch!" and let your child decorate it with Mr. Yuk stickers. (Call your local poison control center or pharmacy to find out where to get the stickers in your area.)

BANDAGE PLAY
This activity helps promote small-muscle development.

1) Make some adhesive "bandages" by cutting masking tape into short strips.
2) Lightly attach the ends of the pretend bandages to the edge of a table or chair seat.
3) Let your child remove the bandages and attach them to himself or herself, to you, or to a stuffed animal.

ANOTHER IDEA: Show your child how to unwrap and apply real adhesive bandages to a knee, a hand, a teddy bear, and so forth.

GOOD-HEALTH CALENDAR
Learning to take care of oneself helps develop self-esteem.

1) Using pen and paper, make a calendar page for one week that includes a space for a picture.
2) With your child, choose a good health habit that you want to practice.
3) Make up a sentence that describes the habit, such as "We eat healthy snacks," and write it on your calendar page.
4) Let your child decorate the calendar with crayons or felt tip markers.
5) At the end of each day, attach two star stickers to your calendar to show that you and your child practiced your good health habit.
6) Each week, make a new calendar page for good habits, such as going to bed on time, washing hands before meals, and getting plenty of exercise.

GAS STATION

I SPY

This color-recognition game is always fun to play.

1) Choose a color such as black.
2) Say, "I spy, with my little eye, a black tire."
3) Ask your child to look out the window (or around the inside of the car) to find another black object, such as a truck.
4) Have your child say, "I spy, with my little eye, a black truck."
5) Continue the game, taking turns naming other black objects.
6) To start a new game, substitute a different color name for black.

OPPOSITE TALK

Try this vocabulary-building activity when you are in the car at the gas station.

1) Talk with your child about opposites as suggested in the sentences below.
   - The driver sits on the left side of the car and the passenger on the right.
   - Roll the windows down, then up.
   - The engine is in the front of the car, and the trunk is in the back.
   - When we clean the windows, they must be closed, not open.
2) Encourage your child to think of other opposites.

GAS STATION

WINDOW CLEANER

This helping activity encourages large-muscle development.

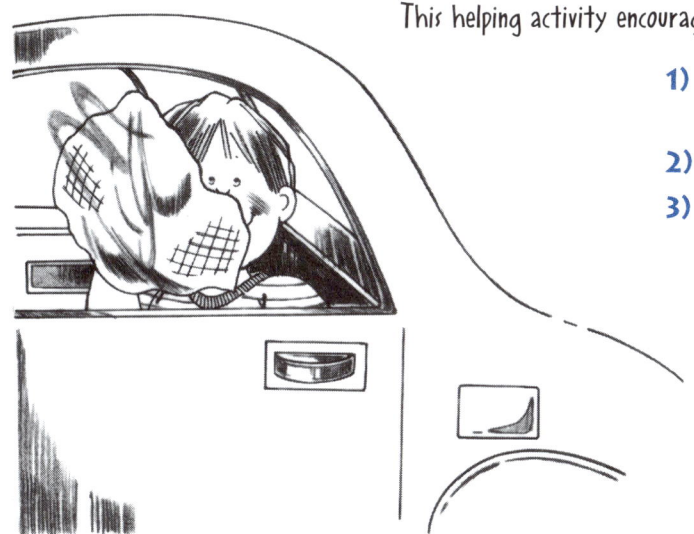

1) Select one of the paper towels at the gas station used for washing windows.
2) Give the dry towel to your child.
3) Let your child use the towel inside the car to "wash" a nearby window, first pretending to squirt on soapy water, then wiping up and down and back and forth with the towel.

FIRST TO LAST

A clean car is what you will have at the end of this sequencing activity.

1) Take your car through the car wash at the gas station.
2) Talk with your child about the order in which things happen, using such examples as the following.
   - First, the car goes into the car wash.
   - Second, the car is sprayed with plain water.
   - Third, the car is scrubbed with soapy water.
   - Fourth, the car is rinsed off.
   - Fifth, the car comes out of the car wash.
3) Later, ask your child to describe what happened at the car wash first, next, and so on.

HOW MUCH?

Your child's self-esteem will blossom when doing this "grown-up" activity.

1) While gas is being pumped into your car, have your child watch the moving numbers on the pump.
2) When the tank is full, point out the numbers that tell how many gallons of gas were pumped and how many dollars they cost.
3) Point to the identification number on the gas pump and name it for your child.
4) Let your child go with you to the cashier, tell the cashier the pump number, and hand him or her the money for the gas.

GAS STATION—AT-HOME FUN

CAR MECHANIC
This dramatic-play activity uses prereading skills.

1) Cut several pictures of cars out of old magazines.
2) Glue the pictures on separate pieces of paper to make pretend work-order forms.
3) Attach the forms to a clipboard and give them to your child.
4) Have your child take the role of garage mechanic while you bring in a toy car to be "repaired."
5) As you name parts of the car for the mechanic to work on, such as a tire and a window, have your child use a pen to mark those parts on a work-order form picture.
6) When the "mechanic" is finished working, have him or her give back the car and "read" the work-order form to you, telling you what repairs were made.
7) Continue the game using other toy cars.

NEIGHBORHOOD CAR WASH
Encouraging large-muscle development is the focus of this activity.

1) Help your child set up a Neighborhood Car Wash on the sidewalk or in your driveway.
2) Hook up a garden hose and set out buckets, rags, and sponges.
3) Have your child invite friends to bring over their riding toys.
4) Let the children use the hose, buckets, rags, and sponges to wash their "cars."

ANOTHER IDEA: Let your child help you wash your car, using just water or a mild soap that is appropriate for young children.

HOMEMADE ROAD MAP
This prereading activity is always a favorite with young children.

1) Show your child a road map from the gas station and talk briefly about how a driver "reads" it.
2) On the floor, place a large piece of paper, such as brown wrapping paper.
3) Assemble some of your child's toy cars.
4) On the paper, use felt tip markers to draw a map with roads wide enough for the toy cars to travel on.
5) Add other details, such as pictures of houses, stores, a park, and a gas station.
6) Let your child "drive" the toy cars on the roads as you give directions such as: "Drive straight ahead to the park. Now turn and drive by the blue house. Stop when you get to the yellow store on the corner."
7) Let your child continue driving cars on the map any way he or she wishes.

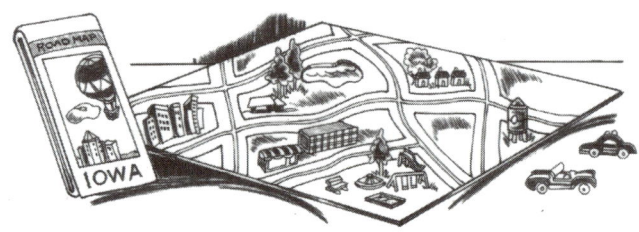